34

Would you like to act out a sexual scene with your partner? What would it look like? What do you want your partner to do or say?

(Role playing)

35

Is the thought of pinning down your lover and holding their wrists while you fuck them exciting? Do you want to be on top and in charge?

(Domination)

36

How would you like to be bent over your partner's knee and spanked? Is it a turn on?

(Spanking)

37

Are you turned on by the idea of squirting? If you're female, have you ever squirted when orgasming?

(Watersports)

38

You're at a party and having a great time. It seems a group of friends have moved into a bedroom and are taking off their clothes. It's obvious they're all about to have sex. Are you interested in joining them?

(Group sex)

39

Do you like it when your lover bites or pinches your nipples? If so, do you prefer it rough or gentle?

(Nipple play)

40

Does the idea of cuddling with your lover while wearing adult diapers and being treated like a baby fascinate you?

(Adult babies)

41

Imagine you walk in late to a movie theater and sit in the back row. There's only one other couple in the theater, and they're sitting in the front row. They don't realize you're there. Before you know it, they're fucking each other loudly. What do you do?

(Voyeurism)

42

Does the idea of being treated like a pet or an animal by your lover turn you on?

(Pet play)

43

Is the idea of multiple people sexually pleasing you at the same time sound hot? Imagine one person after another consecutively fucking you until you're exhausted. Are you turned on?

(Gangbangs)

44

Are you turned on by the idea of using a cucumber or other vegetable as a dildo?

(Food play)

45

Are you interested in wearing leather corsets or shorts?

(Leather play)

46

Have you ever wanted to suck on a lover's toes?

(Foot fetish)

47

Would having your feet and hands bound with rope feel exciting?

(Bondage)

48

You, your partner, and your best friend are hanging out for the evening. On a silly dare, your partner and your friend start making out? What would you like to happen next?

(Swinging)

49

Do you enjoy anal sex? Is it the giving or the receiving that you normally enjoy? Would you be willing to switch it up?

(Anal play or pegging)

50

Do you feel sex is a spiritual experience? Would you like to learn how to prolong the experience and share erotic energy with your partner in more than just a physical sense?

(Tantra)

51

Would you enjoy commanding your lover not to move while you sexually tease them? Is it a turn on to watch them try and obey?

(Domination)

52

If your lover was straddling you naked and the two of you were making out, how would you feel if suddenly they peed all over your lap? Turned on, or turned off?

(Watersports)

53

Does the thought of a lover gently whipping your body with leather straps make you hot and excited?

(BDSM)

54

Do you ever imagine sexy scenarios with your partner in which you both are playing a role? For instance, a "student" has to stay after class with the "teacher"?

(Role playing)

55

If you and your lover were on a beach, lying in the sun and making out, would you get turned on knowing other people were watching the two of you?

(Exhibitionism)

56

Is it erotic to think about your partner comparing you to another lover? What if they were telling you how much better the other person was in bed?

(Cuckolding or Cuckqueaning)

57

How would you like to be blindfolded and commanded by your partner to obey their requests? Would you enjoy being obedient?

(Submission)

58

Is there something sensual or arousing about the thought of struggling while being restrained?

(Bondage)

59

Would you like to be the disciplinarian in a sexual relationship?

(Domination)

60

Does the idea of your lover saying filthy things and swearing during sex turn you on? What would you like to hear them say?

(Dirty talk)

61

Would you like to masturbate in front of your lover (or other people)?

(Exhibitionism)

62

Would you like your partner to use their feet or toes to get you off?

(Foot fetish)

63

Can jealousy or humiliation ever feel sexually arousing?

(Cuckolding or Cuckqueaning)

64

Is wearing a shiny and tight body suit a sexy idea?

(Latex rubber fetish)

65

How would you feel if your partner put a collar and leash on you? What if they made you eat out of a bowl on the ground?

(Pet play)

66

How would you like to feel your lover slide their tongue between your buttocks and lick your anus? Would you like to try it on them too?

(Rimming)

67

Imagine your lover softly caressing a feather all over your naked body while you lie on your back? Would the tickling sensation be a sexual charge?

(Tickling fetish)

68

Do you like rough sex? Is the thought of getting bit and your hair pulled sexually exciting?

(BDSM)

69

Would you like to be woken up to your partner fondling you or giving you oral sex? Does the sight of your sleeping lover sexually excite you?

(Sleep sex)

70

Is it erotic to have sex with your lover while they're fully dressed? How about if you had on all your clothing too?

(Fully clothed fetish)

71

Would it turn you on to watch a couple have sex on security camera footage?

(Voyeurism)

72

Is the idea of a hot, sweaty tangle of people having group sex something that entices you? Have you ever wanted to experience an orgy?

(Group sex)

73

What would you think if you and your partner went on a double date with another couple and everyone ended up in bed together? If you like the idea, is there a couple you could imagine joining you in the bedroom?

(Swinging)

74

Would you like to visit a nude beach or resort?

(Exhibitionism)

75

Is there something primal, erotic, and sexy about fire? Is feeling the warmth of an open flame sensual?

(Fire play)

76

Do you enjoy having your chest massaged or your nipples sucked?

(Nipple play)

77

Is the sensation of wearing spandex or tight, slick clothing a turn-on? Do you enjoy seeing your lover wear items like that?

(Latex rubber fetish)

78

Is it exciting to think about being thrown to the wall and spanked hard?

(BDSM)

79

Do you ever want to see your lover dress the opposite of how they normally would? For instance, a feminine lady dressed in construction worker clothes, or a masculine guy dressed in lingerie?

(Cross-dressing)

80

Do you ever like to pretend your lover is somebody else during sex?

(Role playing)

81

Could referring to your partner as "Sir", "Madam", "Master", or "Mistress" during sex be a turn on to you? Does being "beneath" them feel erotic?

(Submission)

82

Imagine lying naked in bed while lightly restrained and blindfolded. Your partner teases you in a variety of ways and never says a word. Does it sound hot?

(Sensation play)

83

Would you like to be gagged by your lover while they ravish you?

(BDSM)

84

Would you enjoy being disciplined by your lover with a paddle?

(Spanking)

85

Does being fucked from behind with a dildo or penis sound good to you? Does it excite you?

(Anal play or pegging)

86

Have you ever wanted to lick whipped cream off of your lover's body?

(Food play)

87

Imagine having to remain completely silent during sex, no words or sounds. Does it sound like an erotic challenge?

(Silent play)

88

If you and your lover pretended you were complete strangers that met and then had hot passionate sex, would you love it or find it strange?

(Role playing)

89

Have you ever become sexually aroused in the middle of a "tickle fight"?

(Tickling fetish)

90

Do stockings or socks on attractive feet turn you on? How about a sexy person taking off their shoes?

(Foot fetish)

91

If your partner had the ability to give you an electric shock anywhere on your body at will, would you be interested?

(Electrical play)

92

Are you interested in feeling a deeper, more sensual sexual experience with your lover?

(Tantra)

93

Would you be willing to have your hands tied together and hung from the ceiling, your lover teasing your body as you stand there helpless?

(Bondage)

94

How would you like the sensation of a thin rod smacking the bottom of your bare feet?

(Caning)

95

Have you ever enjoyed sex with your lover while both of you are wearing your underwear or panties pushed to the side?

(Fully clothed fetish)

96

Does the thought of making love to your partner in front of a room full of strangers turn you on? If so, describe the most erotic thing about it?

(Exhibitionism)

97

Is it thrilling to imagine having no way of seeing or hearing what your lover may do to you in bed? Every sensation would be a surprise.

(Sensation play)

98

Is the act of urinating ever sexually arousing to you?

(Watersports)

99

Do you ever fantasize about being the complete center of sexual attention in a group of people? All of them are only there to please you. Interested?

(Gangbangs)

100

Do you have your nipples pierced or are you interested in getting them pierced?

(Nipple play)

101

Is it sexually thrilling to imagine getting "punished" in the bedroom by your lover?

(BDSM)

102

Have you ever wanted your partner to slide an ice cube over your naked body?

(Sensation play)

103

Would you be interested in having your partner tell you exactly what to wear in a sexual scenario?

(Submission)

104

Would you like to see someone bigger, stronger, or more attractive than yourself sexually gratify your partner?

(Cuckolding or Cuckqueaning)

105

Is it a turn on to think of your lover groveling as they kneel in front of you? How about making them kiss your feet?

(Domination)

106

Are there any kinks or fetishes not in this book that interest you?

107

Would you like to try any of these kinks we've discussed tonight?

Spice up your love life even more, and explore all the discussion books for couples by J.R. James:

Love and Relationship Books for Couples

Would You Rather...? The Romantic Conversation Game for Couples (Love and Romance Edition)

Sexy Game Books for Couples

Would You Rather...? The Naughty Conversation Game for Couples (Hot and Sexy Edition)

Truth or Dare? The Sexy Game of Naughty Choices (Hot and Wild Edition)

Never Have I Ever... An Exciting and Sexy Game for Adults (Hot and Dirty Edition)

The Hot or Not Quiz for Couples: The Sexy Game of Naughty Questions and Revealing Answers

Pillow Talk: The Sexy Game of Naughty Trivia Questions for Couples

The Naughty Newlywed Game: A Sexy Game of Questions for Couples

Sexy Discussion Books for Couples

Let's Talk Sexy: Essential Conversation Starters to Explore Your Lover's Secret Desires and Transform Your Sex Life

All **THREE** *Let's Talk About...* sexy question books in one massive volume for one low price. Save now!

Let's Talk About... Sexual Fantasies and Desires: Questions and Conversation Starters for Couples Exploring Their Sexual Interests

Let's Talk About... Non-Monogamy: Questions and Conversation Starters for Couples Exploring Open Relationships, Swinging, or Polyamory

Let's Talk About... Kinks and Fetishes: Questions and Conversation Starters for Couples Exploring Their Sexual Wild Side

Change your sex life forever through the power of sexy fun with your spouse, partner, or lover!

www.sexygamesforcouples.com

Sexy Vacations for Couples
https://geni.us/Passion

ABOUT THE AUTHOR

J.R. James is a best-selling author who has a passion for bringing couples closer together and recharging their sexual intimacy. Erotic discussion is a powerfully sexy thing, and his conversation starter books have helped many couples reach new and sexually exciting heights in their relationships!

Sexy conversation with your partner is a magical, bonding experience. Through these best-selling question books, couples can find an easy way to engage in open and honest sexual discussion with each other. The result is a relationship that is both erotically charged and sexually liberating.